Bill Taylor was a miner for thi
in the construction industry,
Safety. He served on Bonnyr
1973, becoming Senior Bailie
Royal Musselburgh golf clubs. ...
he has stayed in Park Crescent since 1940 – during this time, he has moved only four doors along from his original home at number 49. He is a lifelong, ardent supporter of Bonnyrigg Rose Athletic FC.

CW01640740

Typical token drums at a large colliery. As a safety check, miners were issued with two tokens, one to be left with the Banksman before entering the cage for descent, the other to be handed over at the pit bottom before returning to the surface.

My First Day at 'The Lady'

A Scottish Mining Memoir

BILL TAYLOR

PitHead Books

First published 2014

Reprinted 2016

Design by Main Point Books, 77 Bread Street, Edinburgh EH3 9AH
www.mainpointbooks.co.uk

Printed and bound by Bell & Bain Ltd, Glasgow

The paper used in this book is recyclable. It is made from low chlorine pulps produced in a low energy, low emissions manner from renewable forests.

ISBN 978-0-9927233-1-6

© W.F. Taylor 2014

Dedicated to all the men and women of the Scottish mining industry past and present

Contents

Above. Bonnyrigg Toll from Dundas Street with its street light known locally as 'the moon'.

Left: Bill Taylor's grand-parents, Mary and James Macdonald.

An Early Morning Call

It was five am when I got the call to get up. The early morning sun was streaming through the bedroom window and a hen blackbird was darting about the cabbages, picking up caterpillars, probably to feed her hungry brood. The house was alive with people because there were four of us in various stages of getting ready to go out to work. This June morning I was doing it for the first time.

Once I had washed and dressed, the clock was the master, because from Bonnyrigg to Newtongrange was a good four miles and my starting time at the Lady Victoria Colliery was six-thirty am. I couldn't be late. I had walked a 'dummy run' on three occasions over that weekend and I could do it in half an hour. So quarter to six was the latest I could leave the house.

As she had done for more years than she cared to remember, my granny had the 'pieces' made up and the tin flasks filled with tea. One with six sugars, Uncle James. One with four sugars and milk, Uncle Adam. One with no sugar or milk and very weak, Grandfather's. And mine, brand new out of St Cuthbert's hardware, with three sugars and milk.

Each tin flask had a sock bound round it in a different colour for each individual, hand-knitted out of odd bits of wool by the lady of the house. Mine, the newest, was dark blue double knitting – the best Patons and Baldwins.

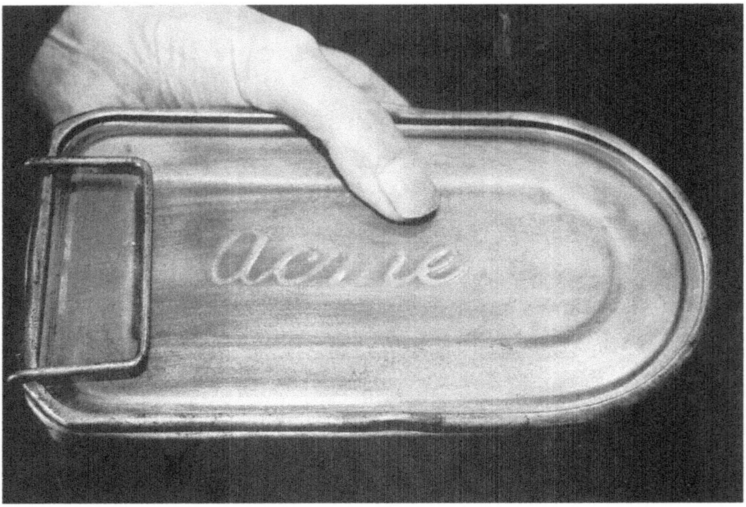

The Acme piece box. Metal and sealed by a strong clip, it protected food taken underground from rats, which spread the potentially fatal Weil's disease.

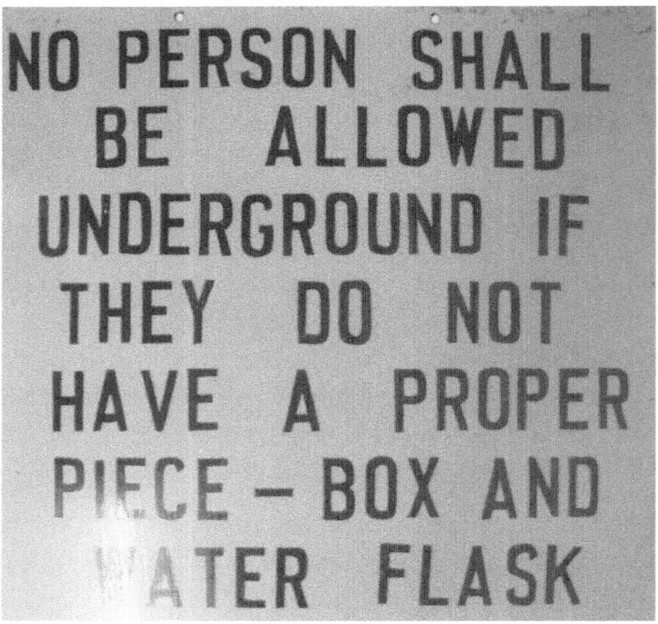

Pit-head notice. Spot searches ensured compliance.

The Pit Piece

The 'piece' was wrapped in the *Daily Herald* and put in an Acme tin box, the shape of a plain loaf, bought from the store's hardware department for 1/3d. So for piece box and flask I was half a crown in debt, with the cost of the hob-nailed boots to be added. My first pay was just about spoken for.

The pit piece, I was to learn very quickly, was a bit of a status symbol at work amongst the miners. How can slices of plain bread become a status symbol? You may well ask. Well, it was like this. When 'piece time' came, the conversation centred on what was between the slices of bread and what was spread on them. Simple? Not so.

My grandfather always maintained that you could tell a man's occupation in any pit by the piece he brought with him. He even went as far as to suggest he could tell whether the owner was a 'genuine' miner or one of these Bevin Boys who had come in to skip the Forces during the Second World War – which was not really true, as they were 'pressed' men with little choice in the matter.

My grandfather was a machineman, the most skilled job at the coalface, manoeuvring a six ton, twelve foot eighteen inches high, solid piece of good Scottish engineering in the three feet hard Splint Coal Seam, along a 250-foot track. It could be an easy four feet undercut or the jib of the machine could hit the notorious ‘bullets’ on its path. These ironstone intrusions into the seam had to be hand-picked out, before the machine could make progress. So the machine team, who had seven hours before the colliers came on shift, might have to work shift without a break to eat, in which case their piece would be handed on to a tub-runner or switchman as the team left the section.

So a machineman’s piece was economical to say the least: Co-op margarine and home-made or Co-op mixed fruit jam. The plus for this, according to my grandfather, was that it was easy to digest. I don’t know what modern-day medical opinion would say about that bit of philosophy.

Grandfather maintained that a cheese or spam piece spread with butter was brought by men who had little physical work to do – for example, belt-switchmen or surveyors, who made weekly visits to measure roadway advances, who had plenty time to eat it during their shift.

The other distinction Grandfather made between the ‘workers’ and the ‘servers’, so to speak, was the number of slices: ‘workers’ not more than two; ‘casuals’ up to six. Age also had to be taken into account. The older you were, the less you brought, whereas a fifteen-year-old needed all his six slices and anybody else’s that was going spare. Nothing changes when it comes to young appetites.

Six slices of plain white loaf were the most you could get into an Acme piece tin. So, with two slices of toast and a cup of tea in me, my piece and flask in my army surplus haversack, gleaming steel toe-capped boots on my feet, new pit-head bath towel and soap, working jeans, blue hairy shirt, blue vest and pants and old jacket, all wrapped up together and tied with a leather belt, and an old bunnet on my head, it was out the door and heading for the Cockpen Road, striding it out to ‘The Lady’ tables – a working man in full regalia, away to earn his first day’s pay.

The Waverley Hotel, Bonnyrigg, where Bill Taylor was born in 1937.

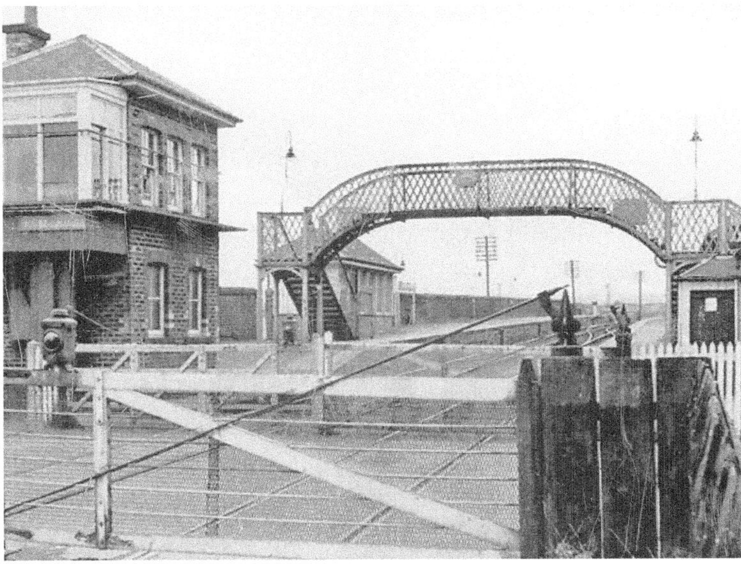

The Edinburgh–Peebles line crossing at Bonnyrigg Station.

From Park Crescent I turned into Bonnyrigg High Street, where groups of men were standing at Allan Forrest's grocer's shop, waiting for the bus for Loanhead (the Ramsay or Burghlee Colleries) or for Roslin (the 'Moat', my grandfather's and uncle's pit). Jibes of 'Lift yer feet', 'Are you away to work for Mungie Mackay?' and 'Traitor!' were soon ringing in my ears.

An explanation is needed for the jibes that were good-humouredly shouted at me.

The Loanhead and Roslin pits were formerly owned by the Shotts Iron Company, and 'The Lady' by the Lothian Coal Company under the dreaded 'Mungie Mackay', a general manager who was seen as a bit of a tyrant by people in the district because of the rigid discipline he imposed on his workers, who all lived locally in Company houses. The fact that he had been dead nearly twenty years, or that the pits were now owned by the National Coal Board and 'managed on behalf of the people' did not make any difference to the miners that morning or any other morning.

I went through the Toll with its big light in the centre of the crossroads, past Mennel's paper shop and the Calderwood Arms, then down to the Waverley Hotel, where I was born fifteen years before, and across the tracks of the Edinburgh–Peebles railway line. On the platform, waiting on the first train to Peebles, were the local pigeon fanciers Dave Burnett and Bobby Bryce, who were sending their 'Rennes birds' to Peebles for a 'toss' before they went 'across the water' at 'the Trades' holiday (the first fortnight in July) for the 'big race'. They would send their birds on that trip to Peebles every morning for a fortnight, even though it cost 1/- a time. The birds were let off by the guard and the baskets brought back on the return journey.

On either side of the Cockpen Road, Barr's fields of barley were swaying gently in the early morning breeze; swaths were caught in the sunlight, giving the impression of golden waves.

Cockpen Church.

I caught up with three older men who were travelling to the same destination, Davie Law, a local wag who I was to see plenty of in the next six months, and Jim Kay and Bobby Moody, who I knew as 'West Country men' – miners who had transferred from Lanarkshire in the late forties and early fifties.

A grunt of recognition was all I got as I bade them good-morning, before strolling on past Cockpen school and the tower of Martin of George Street's house.

A tractor was making its way from lower Dalhousie Farm and two black and white collies gave me a bark as they chased each other in the field.

Over the brow of the hill, on my right, Cockpen Church and churchyard stood like a beacon of the past as I headed for the crossroads that would tell me I was halfway to my destination.

Butlerfield marshalling yards at Lady Victoria Colliery.

The entrance to Lady Victoria Colliery *c.* 1954.

Nature's Playground

I went through the crossroads and up past The Glen, a playground for many generations in the district to live out the big movie fantasies of Tyrone Power and Roy Rogers. A stream ran through The Glen, making its way to the South Esk. In the sky above me, birds swooped around, enjoying the morning sunshine. I felt like an intruder into nature's playtime.

Dalhousie Castle, the home of the Ramsays, now came into view in all its eleventh-century majesty, reflecting, with the almost as old chestnut trees, on its past. It was now a school for colonial administrators' sons, who were kept very much within the confines of the magnificent estate.

At ten past six I reached Butlerfield Cottages and 'The Lady' came into view, with its great plumes of steam from the winding engine vanishing into the morning sky above Newtongrange.

The shunting pugs were busy to-ing and fro-ing in the big marshalling yards with wagons of coal from the washery, the old red livery of the Lothian Coal Company making a fine splash of colour against sidings black with derailed coal.

Turning the corner at Allan's Garage and the Auld Toll, I walked down towards the Victorian buildings that were the hub of the National Coal Board's administration for the Newbattle group of collieries – Lady Victoria, Lingerwood and Easthouses.

As I passed the offices, the thing that struck me was the numbers over each window: 1–499, 500–999 and so on, with times 8.30am–9.30am, 9.45am–10.30am etc. Strange at the time, but all would be revealed, and remembered, very soon because that was where and when you were paid on a Friday if you worked backshift or nightshift at Lady Victoria, Easthouses and Lingerwood. Pay day was a fortnight away for me.

For a week's work I would receive the princely sum of £5 10d, less the standard deductions for National Insurance, the Miners' Welfare Fund and a penny each for the local pipe and silver bands. We also donated a penny to St Andrew's Ambulance Association, a body that I was to have a thirty-plus years' association with. They were the approved body that taught miners first aid and ran local and national competitions for the industry.

The big question to come with my pay packet was: was it pocket money, or would I have to pay my grandmother for my digs? The answer, for a few years until my wages were sufficient, was pocket money.

The Pit-head Baths

Up the pit road to the baths I went. A huge building, constructed with bricks from the Lingerwood brickworks, proudly proclaimed its name and showed the crest of the National Coal board above the entrance. Through the revolving doors I came into a tiled hall where some men loitered having a smoke before they entered Peter Roberts' empire. Peter was the baths superintendant, all powerful in his spick-and-span domain. 'Name?' – he barked.

I was assigned Locker 837. Thrust before me was a Bather's Slip to sign, upon which I became the recipient of a numbered key and a Bather's Handbook. 'Read that and you won't get into bother,' I was told.

Slowly moving from locker bank to locker bank, I came to the bay with Locker 837. I peered at the numbers below and above until I came to mine. My locker was on the bottom.

'Got a bottom yin, have ye? Ye must be in the know,' said a half-naked man from behind an open door.

'No,' said I in all innocence, 'it's the one the man gave me.'

Stripped, clean clothes into the locker, towel round me and still in tackety boots, then round to the 'dirty side' to put on my working clothes and leave my towel and soap for the end of the shift. You may ask why I didn't get dressed in my

At the coalface.

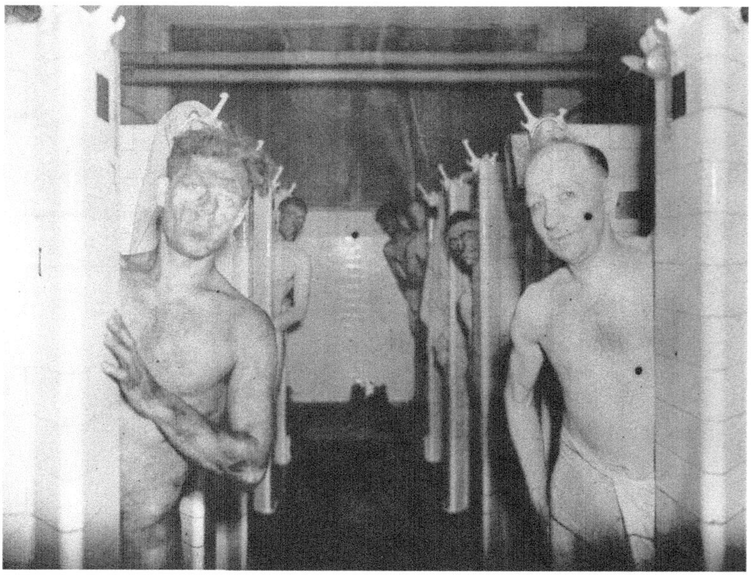

End of shift, in the showers.

working clothes at the 'clean side' but that was not allowed, despite the fact that they were in mint condition. Shadows of Mungie Mackay, maybe, but not really – the clean side *meant* the clean side and this was respected by all miners.

From the dirty side, I made my way across the concrete gantry that stretched from the baths to the pit-head, crossing forty feet above the A7 Edinburgh to Galashiels Road, to the Token Hall. I was completely oblivious to the swarms of men coming towards me having finished the nightshift, black and wet looking, moving forward to the hot showers.

The token office was brightly lit, with men shouting numbers and hands thrusting brass, coin-like objects into outstretched hands with military precision, without breaking stride.

I reported to the surface window, showed my bath key and was given my tokens and then I made my way by following the arrows to the 'tables'.

Above: The picking table at the Lady Victorie *c*. 1953.

Left: Bill Taylor outside 'The Tables' enjoying piece time.

The Tables

Coming out of the bustle of the Token Office into the sunlight and across a ribbed iron gantry, past the cage, a vista of smoking fires and long, steel, belt-like structures met my eyes, all stopped and silent, because the pit was winding men. The silence was soon to be shattered when the pit hooter went at half past six, and coal tubs came up from the depths of the earth to spew their contents onto these moving iron monsters.

A group of people were standing around a fire enclosed in an old forty-five-gallon oil drum, listening to a huge man who spat out instructions between draws at his pipe. This was a man I was to know as the 'Pit-head Gaffer': Big Will Reid, an autocrat with a heart of gold if you came from 'Nitten' and supported The Star, the local football team. Big Will was a man who had lived and worked under the most severe of coalmasters and had had to come out of the pit because of bad health. Because he had been a very hard worker, the company had given him a job on the surface, a privilege hard-earned under the old coal owners.

'Where ye goin, ma man?' he barked, spotting me intruding on his domain.

'I have to report to the pit-head gaffer for a job. It's all been arranged by Mr Mabon, the Training Officer.'

'Mr Mabon disnae arrange anything for the washer, he only

sends folk and I dae the arranging if they're suitable. What's yer name?'

By this time I was reliving *Oliver Twist* because it felt as if I had moved back in time to the Victorian era.

'Bill Taylor,' I said, half-choking.

'Speak up, man. Ye'll have to speak louder than that when the tables start. But ye'll learn.'

He drew out a dirty book, thumbed through it and said, 'Report to table eleven, the Parrot Table. But before ye go, a few things to remember. Starting time's half past six, piece time is eleven o'clock, lousing time is four o'clock. A see ye want to go doon the pit, then ye must never be late in the morning – never lose a shift – an dae whit yer telt. I'll review your position in six months' time.'

Having had my 'induction', I moved away along the lines of picking tables, which were numbered and had names on them like Great Seam, Coronation Dook, Cannel, Easthouses and Splint, until I came to number eleven, 'Parrot'. Lo and behold, standing at the head of the conveyor, leaning on the handle that operated the pivot to load the coal into the awaiting wagons some ten feet below, was the man I'd passed on the Cockpen Road that morning. Davie Law.

'Well, Macdonald,' he said (I was known as Macdonald because that was my grandparents' name and I stayed with them during and after the war), 'A kent ye were coming the day and a asked for ye, okay.'

At last, a friendly face, I thought. He proceeded to hand me a ten-pound hammer and gesticulated towards the largest pile of white rock I had seen in my life, and said, 'You are on the red pile, aw that goes through that grid into the wagon below – get on with it – a'll tell ye when it's piece time.' Then it felt as if all hell was let loose because the pit hooter went off wailing, and almost simultaneously all eleven steel picking tables started up in unison with a grinding and screeching. There were dozens of people on each side of the tables, picking stones and other materials from the black mass on them until only clean coal went into the wagons. These tables went from starting time till two pm, when they started to wind men up the pit, and restarted for the backshift at three o'clock. The noise was deafening.

I was taken aback to see women and girls working at the picking tables. I later learned that they were there to keep a roof over their heads because the family breadwinner had suffered some accident, rendering him unable to work. If there were no sons available to take up employment, it fell to the women to earn enough to pay the weekly rent. Women also worked in the Company brickworks.

At the tables, my pile was being added to by the minute as I started wielding the hammer up and down, up and down continuously, and did that till I was tapped on the shoulder and told, 'Go for your piece.' When I came back twenty minutes later it was as if I had never been away. Even when they stopped winding coal at two o'clock I was still at it, trying to get rid of it down the hole.

It took me weeks to learn that it never totally disappeared, because there were only so many wagons allocated to dirt each day. Dirt didn't make money, coal did, so coal got priority.

At four o'clock we finished and meandered back through the Token Office and along the gantry to the baths. I got out of my working clothes and into that hot shower. I felt like staying under it forever as the water soothed the first aches of working life.

Mining collage created By Andy Walstall for the National Mining Museum of Scotland.

Davie Law, the 'Law Man' – a dream fulfilled: Bonnyrigg win the Scottish Junior Cup in 1966.

Homeward Bound

Once dressed, I made my way out of the baths entrance and who did I see but my supervisor and fellow Park Crescent resident Davie Law, sucking away at his trusty old pipe. On spotting me he said, 'Macdonald, if you take this long in the showers they will start charging you for water and you will be walking home on your own.' We strolled out of the pit yard, homeward bound along the reverse route I had taken that morning, full of enthusiasm to be a working man. But now, much tireder and wiser, it took me twice as long to make my way home; it was head down all the way and I don't remember seeing anything that I had noticed in the morning.

The 'Law Man', as Davie was affectionately known locally, was a diehard Bonnyrigg Rose FC supporter. He looked after the playing kit, which was transported everywhere the team played in a huge wicker basket. If you were 'in the know with Davie' he would let us young ones help him carry it. It weighed a ton but we saw this as a great honour and he was not short of volunteers, because you also got into the game for nothing for being part of the Kit Team. Davie's dream was that his beloved Rose would win the Holy Grail of junior football, the Scottish Cup (he twice saw his dream come true, with thousands of other supporters, in 1966 and 1978).

When we reached Park Crescent we went our separate ways to our respective abodes.

In the stair at number 49, the aroma of lentil soup met my nostrils and I knew that my dinner was ready. I was ready for it! I felt like Desperate Dan and had his appetite, or so I thought at the time.

'How did it go?' was the greeting from my grandmother.

'Great,' said I, feeling a numbness coming into muscles I never knew I had. 'I'm working with Davie Law.'

'Oh, that's fine, he'll look after you,' she replied, filling my soup plate with the large enamel label that had been a wedding present and was used most days. 'Sit down, you'll be ready for this.'

A plate of lentil soup – two ends of a plain loaf – then mince and tatties were put down in front of me and vanished without a word being said.

I left the table and went straight to bed and never woke up until I heard that familiar voice at five am, and day two was about to start, with the same routine all laid out before me for the next six months.

The six months flew in and my body adjusted to the noise and the manual rigours of lifting stones and other discard from the tables. One day I got the call I was waiting for from the Training Officer. I was going on my underground training for three months, then off to Easthouses pit to be a real miner.

My first day there was a great contrast to my introduction to the industry at 'The Lady'. From working in a large group on the surface picking tables, with acres of space around us, I found myself under close personal supervision, over a thousand feet underground, in a narrow, small-arched roadway in the Return Airway of the mine.

Underground training was a real eye-opener: the emphasis was on gaining the necessary skills and understanding how vital team-work was; working safely in every task was of paramount importance. Our trainers had been there and done it all. They were now passing on that experience to trainees in the working environment. This was only the start of the long learning journey I was about to undertake in the industry.

I will always remember the men who trained me. They asked for nothing in return for their mentoring skills and while they seldom praised you to your face, when you succeeded in anything academically, they let their peers know that they were pleased to have contributed in a small way.

It has been a great privilege to have know men like Jimmy Allan, Willie Conlan, John Aitchison, 'Old' McSeveney, the Nicol Brothers, Harry Thomson, Alex Grierson, Pat Moonie, John Hughes, Willie Steel and Tommy Gray. They taught lessons of life that money cannot buy. Years later, some incident or conversation would often bring them back into my thoughts.

These men subtly instilled in young miners a pride in their work and the value of serving their community. Older miners at Easthouses persuaded me to attend night school to learn more about the industry and in so doing, laid the foundations for my career in mining and my trade union activities.

One thing is certain, I have never had any regrets about the decision I made to start in the industry that gave me a good education and living for thirty-five years.

Bath-time in a miner's cottage before the installation of pit-head baths at collieries (an exhibit at the National Mining Museum of Scotland).

Typical miners row: Fourth Street, Newtongrange. These are two-bedroom houses but many Company houses had only one bedroom and no indoor toilet.

Note on the Lady Victoria Colliery

From its outset, Lady Victoria Colliery – 'The Lady' – was the jewel of the Scottish coalfields. The sinking of the shaft commenced in August 1890 and was completed in 1894. The total final depth was around 500 metres. The shaft sinking was not without a human cost, with two men losing their lives.

The shaft site in Newtongrange was chosen because it was central to the rich Midlothian coalfield basin. Another consideration was that it was near another colliery owned by the Lothian Coal Company, Lingerwood. This saved the Company sinking another Statutory second shaft, a costly business. A big plus for the location was that it was adjacent to the busy Edinburgh–Hawick railway line, giving the Company access to additional markets in Edinburgh and the emerging Borders textile industry. The vast railway sidings at Butlerfield were necessary to despatch and receive materials for the colliery.

Underground, the Company was fortunate to be able to work to the 'rise' in the coal seam, which mean that all roadway drivages followed the contours of the seam from the shaft bottom; another plus for working this way was that any water encountered ran away from the production face. Around 120 pit ponies worked underground before mechanical haulage systems were introduced in the 1920s. The Company had its own brickworks, which were part and parcel of many pits. Clay was also mined as part of the coal-getting process.

At its peak, The Lady employed around 1,700 people from the Lothians and Edinburgh. Following the 1912 Miners' Strike, the miners' rows in Newtongrange were cited by the Royal Commission on Housing in Scotland as a model village, 'probably the best built for miners in Scotland'. Nonetheless, families of up to eight lived in two-bedroom houses with no internal toilet facilities (the 'lavvy' was situated at the bottom of the garden and emptied by the Company contractor once a week).

The inhabitants all worked for the Company. If a miner was fired, failed to keep the garden up to scratch or broke Company rules, the whole family became homeless. My grandfather's family suffered this fate at the Lothian Coal Company pit at Whitehill in Rosewell, over a wages dispute. The workers who withdrew their labour were also blacklisted for employment.

The 'rows' were alive with children. Street games abounded, with football always popular with the boys. Many famous Scottish footballers emerged from the mining villages, including Jock Stein, Jock Wallace, Bill Shankly and Willie Bauld, and two Newtogrange Star players Davie McKay (Tottenham Hotspur) and Alex Young (Heart of Midlothian and Everton).

At the annual village gala day the 'Queen' was crowned and, led by the local silver and pipe bands, everyone paraded through the village to the park to continue the festivities. Many former mining villages continue these traditions to this day.

Life was very hard in the rows, but despite this there was a strong sense of sharing and community spirit.

The Lady Victoria Colliery pioneered many techniques in the mechanisation of coal production and coal transport systems. The last wagon of coal was mined there in 1981 and the site is now the Scottish National Mining Museum. Its unique, Scottish-built winding engine is still in motion today for visitors to see and hear.

Any miner committing a misdemeanour had to 'stand before the green table' where Company justice was dispensed.

The last tubs of coal mined in the Lady Victoria, 1981.

Lady Victoria head gear.

Glossary of Mining Terms

Bevin Boy: A person who did his conscripted National Service in the coal mines rather than in the Armed Forces, between 1943 and 1960.

Coalface: The exposed area of a coal seam from which coal is extracted either manually or by machine.

Coalcutter: A machine used to undercut at the coalface. There are many types, from chain or jib machines up to the modern disc shearer drum machine.

Colliery Training Officer: A suitably qualified and experienced individual, appointed by the mine manager under the Mines and Quarries Act, to ensure in his behalf that all persons employed in the mine were adequately trained and supervised.

Conveyor: A continuous moving belt or chain that transported large volumes of material.

Hutch: A wooden or metal car used to carry coal and other materials within mine workings. (Hutches are know outwith Scotland as 'tubs'.)

Machineman: The person who operated the machine that undercut the coal seam before it was blasted and physically loaded onto a coalface conveyor, then onto a 'roadway' conveyor and then into 'hutches' or 'tubs' for transporting to the surface.

Miners' Welfare Fund 1920: A government levy on mine owners of one penny per ton was introduced in 1920 to set up a fund for the purpose of enhancing the recreational and living conditions of mine workers in and around collieries. In 1926 the levy was increased by

At the Lady Victoria, the lockers were steam-cleaned monthly.

Underground Training Gallery safety notices.

one penny to fund the construction of pit-head baths; other surface facilities such as first aid, ambulance and medical training schemes came under its remit. It was used to fund community facilities that included Miners' Institutes, libraries and reading rooms for the free use of the community; the Fund supported social and cultural activities such as music, drama and literature and helped to establish Mining Departments in colleges.

Picking Table: Flat or slightly sloping metal conveyor onto which raw coal and other materials were tipped to be sorted by individual 'pickers'.

Pit-head baths: A building containing showers and designated changing areas with personal lockers. They were provided by the Miners' Welfare Fund 1920, for miners to wash after their shift at a time when miners' houses did not have baths or showers.

Pit-head 'Gaffer': A person appointed by the manager of the mine to supervise surface activities such as the picking tables, the materials compound etc.

Redd: A commonly used term used to describe all waste and stone generated by the coal-cleaning process on the surface.

Switchman: The person who controlled the stopping and starting of the 'roadway' conveyors that transported the coal to the surface.

Token or Check Office: An office, close to or on the way to the pit-head, from which each colliery employee was issued with two numbered brass tokens (or tags) for personal identification at the beginning of every shift. These tokens had a number unique to the individual all his working life in that colliery. Its return at the end of a shift ensured that every employee was accounted for.

Tub Runner: Person responsible for ensuring that the filled and empty 'hutches' (or 'tubs') were kept moving on the underground rail system and surface rail layout. Tub-making was a skilled job undertaken in the surface waggon-shops.

L to R: Bill Taylor, Cousin Albert, Aunt Mary (Pelligrinetti), Grandfather James Macdonald and Cousin Kerry.

Some Family History

My mother, Anne (née Macdonald), was born in Bo'ness and my father, William, the son of a railway engineer, was born in Doncaster in the early 1900s. Both worked in service, and that was probably how they met each other. In 1937 they were working in a country house in Dorset, where William doubled up as chef and driver. At that time my maternal grandparents, Mary (née Fulton) and James Macdonald were living in Bonnyrigg and when they realised I was on the way, my parents decided that I should be born in Scotland, and so my mother travelled north for the birth.

My grandparents started married life in Bo'ness, West Lothian. After serving with the 8th/9th Royal Scots in the First World War, James became a merchant seaman – there was a good trade with Russia and Finland for timber, mainly for the mining industry, but with the downturn in the economy in the 1920s the trade declined; he then worked in Furnace Yards No. 4 Pit in Bo'ness (later Kinneill Colliery).

After the 1926 Miners' Strike, my grandparents moved to Rosewell where James had obtained work as a Machineman in Whitehill Colliery. Following a dispute about wages at Whitehill, James lost his job and his Company house. A Bonnyrigg farmer, Willie Pringle, kindly gave them spare cottage he had until they secured better accommodation.

William Taylor Snr in army uniform, 1940.

The cottage was pretty basic accommodation and quite a squeeze a family of eight, so they then moved into two rooms in the Waverley Hotel in Dundas Street, Bonnyrigg. (Although called a 'hotel', the Waverley had long since ceased to function in that fashion and now rented out its rooms. It still exists as a public house.) It was at the Waverley that I was born on 8th October, 1937.

Some weeks later, after having me baptised in Cockpen Kirk, my mother rejoined my father and we were together as family for my first Christmas.

While still at the Waverley Hotel, my grandfather started work at the Moat Colliery, Roslin, which was owned by the Shotts Iron Company, a far more progressive outfit than the Lothian Coal Company which then owned Whitehill Colliery and Lady Victoria. In 1938 my grandparents were rehoused by the council at 49 Park Crescent where they spent the rest of their days.

After serving in the Second World War, their three sons – Ranald, James and Adam – also worked in the mining industry, two at Roslin and one at Burghlee. My Uncle James delved into family genealogy, but unfortunately whatever he found out has been lost, but I do remember him saying that my grandmother originally came from Sleat on the Isle of Skye. I certainly remember her speaking in Gaelic with her two sisters, and they used to attend the Gaelic services at Greyfriars Kirk in Edinburgh.

~

Early in the Second World War my father was called up and the mansion where he and my mother worked was requisitioned by the War Department. Despite the bombing of London, my mother moved in with her elder sister, Mary, in Hampstead, and not long after was conscripted to work for the war effort.

During the London Blitz of 1940, many children were separated from their families and sent to live in the country for their safety. Officially registered as a 'refugee', I was consigned to Scotland and the safe hands of my grandparents in Bonnyrigg, with my 'tinny' (a wee enamel mug), gas mask and refugee label. Not yet four, I was put on the night train from King's Cross to Waverley and then on to Broomieknowe Station. The last part of my journey was in the guard's van – the early train to Polton Paper Mill had no passenger carriages because the mill manufactured bank-note paper and the train was specially designated for its secure transport. I was excited to meet the train driver, a Bonnyrigg man called Dick Skirving,

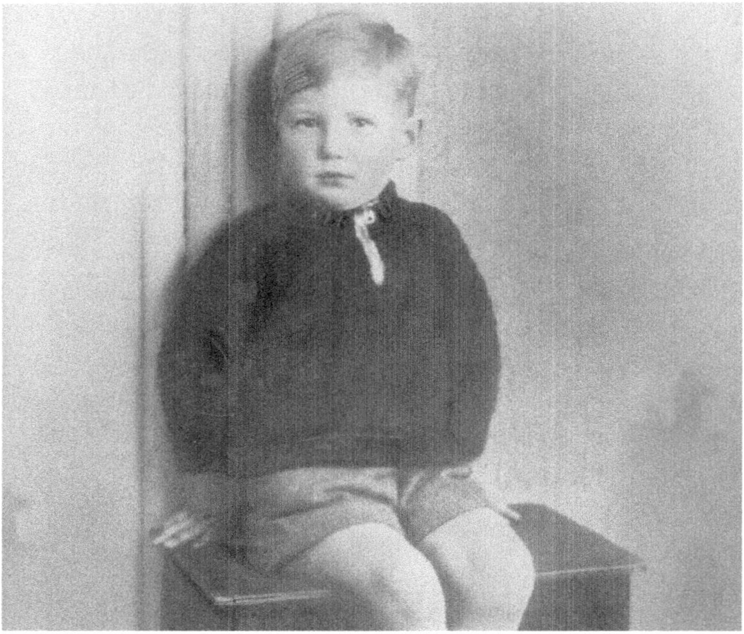

The young 'refugee' – Bill Taylor aged four.

Infant Class, Bonnyrigg Primary School, 1942.

who knew my family. In 1941 my Aunt Mary and her sons Albert and Terry also came to live in Bonnyrigg.

At five years of age, in December 1942, I was enrolled at Bonnyrigg Infants' School. I remember going through the gates hand-in-hand with George Crawford, who became a friend for life (incidentally, he came from a family of twenty-three and like me he later went into the mining industry).

The two Infant teachers, Miss Bell and Miss Steel, were strict but they were also kind; they instilled in us discipline and manners, and respect for our elders. They were both local to Bonnyrigg and played a big part in community life down the generations – they were still at the school when my son entered the Infants in the 1960s.

Even after the war ended, I stayed on with my grandparents, my three uncles and my youngest aunt, Ina. My parents had returned to Dorset where they found work in a new hotel and I saw nothing of them during my school days, but I later visited them frequently. They died some twenty years ago.

I attended Bonnyrigg Junior Secondary School, and left at fifteen with a School Leaving Certificate in six subjects. It was time to find a job. The last place my grandfather wanted me to work was in the mines. In the post-war era, there were plenty opportunities in engineering and construction, but I didn't fancy any of these and unbeknown to him I applied for a job in the pits. During the three-month waiting period till I got my call to go for a medical, I took a job as a tea-boy on a building site. Having passed Medical Grade 1, I was allocated to the surface of Lady Victoria Colliery, where my adventure with the coal industry started in earnest.

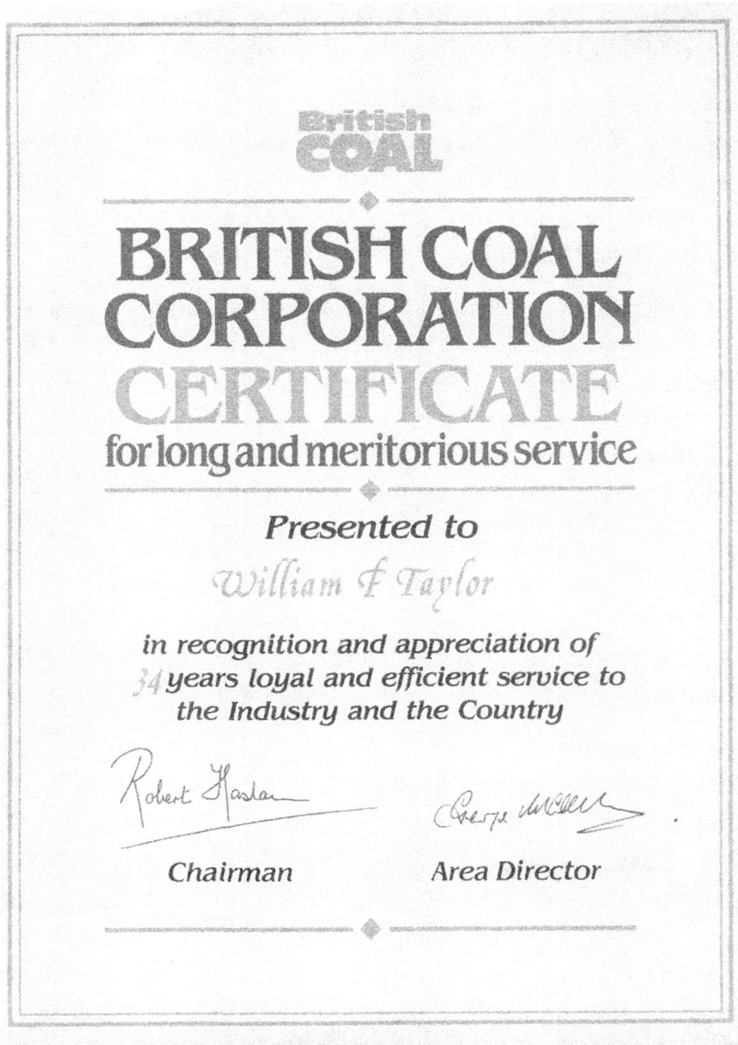

British COAL

BRITISH COAL CORPORATION

CERTIFICATE

for long and meritorious service

Presented to

William F Taylor

in recognition and appreciation of 34 years loyal and efficient service to the Industry and the Country

Chairman

Area Director

Chronology of Bill Taylor's Working Life

1953 Surface worker Lady Victoria Colliery.

1954 Started underground Easthouses Colliery General oncost and faceworker.

1960 Won a TUC Education Trust Scholarship to study Politics, Economics and Industrial Law at London School of Economics.

1962 Returned to Easthouses Colliery as faceworker.

Resumed Mining Studies at Dalkeith High School and Esk Valley College in the old Nissen huts, Stobhill.

1964 NCB Industrial Relations Trainee Scheme, Ayrshire.

1966 Assistant Manpower Officer, Fife.

1968 Assistant Industrial Relations Officer, Department of Manpower and Industrial Training, Lothians.

1968 Assistant Manager Personnel, Bilston Glen Colliery.

1977 Industrial Training Officer, Education, Scottish Area NCB.

1981 Head of Industrial Training, British Coal Scotland.

1986 Head of Manpower and Industrial Training, British Coal Scotland.

1988 Left British Coal Scotland at coalfield reorganisation.

1989 Training Manager, University of Edinburgh.

1990 Training and Industrial Relations Officer, Electrical Contractors' Association of Scotland.

1992 Studied at Stevenson College for a Diploma in Health and Safety.

Appointed Health and Safety Advisor for Electrical Contractors' Association of Scotland.

1992 Lectured and advised member companies on Health and Safety legislation (until 2002).

Received diplomas from the European Health and Safety Commission.

1998 Lectured on Manual Handling techniques for care homes and retail outlets.

2001 Primary Schools Initiative – arranged children's educational visits to local construction sites.

2002 Asbestos Awareness Initiative – advising and lecturing on the dangers of asbestos in the workplace.

2003 Retired from full-time work aged 65.

Bill Taylor with his European Union Health and Safety Award at the Dorchester Hotel, London, March 2002.

Acknowledgements

The publication of this memoir was made possible by the generous help of many people, in particular Alex Watson and Lynsey Anderson of the Mining Museum of Scotland, Lady Victoria, who allowed reproduction of images from the museum's photographic collection. I am also grateful to the Midlothian Libraries Local History service for use of the image of Bonnyrigg Toll and to Cockpen and Carrington Church Board for permission to reproduce the image of Cockpen Church. I wish to thank John Ferguson, Oscar Ramage and Jennie Renton for designing and creating this book.